1 MONTH OF
FREE
READING

at
www.ForgottenBooks.com

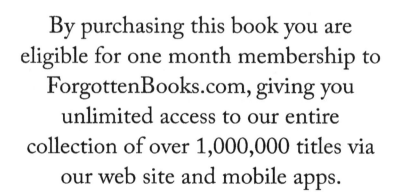

By purchasing this book you are eligible for one month membership to ForgottenBooks.com, giving you unlimited access to our entire collection of over 1,000,000 titles via our web site and mobile apps.

To claim your free month visit:
www.forgottenbooks.com/free168415

ISBN 978-0-260-83740-0
PIBN 10168415

BRITISH WAR FRONTS

VOLUMES ILLUSTRATED BY MARTIN HARDIE, A.R E

OUR ITALIAN FRONT

Described by H WARNER ALLEN   With 50 full-page illustrations in colour, and a sketch map   Square demy 8vo , cloth
Price 25s. net.

BOULOGNE: A WAR BASE IN FRANCE

Containing 32 reproductions—8 in colour and 24 in sepia—
from drawings completed on the spot. Square demy 8vo,
cloth. **Price 7s. 6d. net.**

OTHER VOLUMES

THE SALONIKA FRONT

Painted by WILLIAM T WOOD, R.W.S. Described by CAPTAIN
A J MANN, R A F   With 32 full-page illustrations in colour,
and 8 in black and white, also a sketch map   Square demy
8vo , cloth **Price 25s. net.**

THE NAVAL FRONT

**A Book dealing with the world-wide front held by the British
Navy throughout the war**

By LIEUT GORDON S MAXWELL, R N V R, Illustrated in
colour by LIEUT DONALD MAXWELL, R N V R   Containing
32 full page illustrations, 16 of them in colour   Square demy
8vo , cloth *In Preparation.*

THE IMMORTAL GAMBLE

And the part played in it by H M S. "Cornwallis."

By A T STEWART, Acting-Commander, R.N.. and the REV
C J E. PESHALL, Chaplain, R.N. With 32 illustrations and
a map. **Price 6s net ; now offered at 3s. 6d. net.**

MERCHANT ADVENTURERS, 1914-1918

By F A HOOK With a Foreword by the Rt Hon. LORD
INCHCAPE OF STRATHNAVER, G C M C, G C.S I., etc. Containing 32 full-page illustrations from photographs, and
appendixes. Large crown 8vo., cloth.

In the Press.

PUBLISHED BY
A. AND C. BLACK, LTD , 4, 5 AND 6 SOHO SQUARE LONDON, W I

WAR POSTERS

ISSUED BY BELLIGERENT AND NEUTRAL NATIONS 1914-1919

SELECTED & EDITED BY
MARTIN HARDIE AND
ARTHUR K. SABIN

A. & C. BLACK, LTD.
SOHO SQUARE, LONDON, W.

1920

TO

FRANK PICK, Esq.,

OF THE UNDERGROUND ELECTRIC RAILWAYS COMPANY,

IN HONOUR OF HIS BRAVE AND SUCCESSFUL EFFORT

TO LINK ART WITH COMMERCE

CONTENTS

CHAPTER I.

CHAPTER II.

CHAPTER III.

CHAPTER IV.

CHAPTER V.

CHAPTER VI.

LIST OF ILLUSTRATIONS

ARRANGED UNDER THE NAMES OF ARTISTS AND GROUPED UNDER THE COUNTRIES OF ISSUE

Illustrations marked with an asterisk (*) are in colour.

8. GERALD SPENCER PRYSE.

> THE ONLY ROAD FOR AN ENGLISHMAN. THROUGH DARKNESS TO LIGHT; THROUGH FIGHTING TO TRIUMPH. The first war poster by Spencer Pryse   Published by the Underground Electric Railways Company of London, 1914.

9. GERALD SPENCER PRYSE.

> BELGIAN REFUGEES IN ENGLAND. Issued by the Belgian Red Cross Fund in London, 1915.

10. GEORGE CLAUSEN, R.A.

> "MINE BE A COT BESIDE THE HILL." This poster was one of a group of four which were sent out by the Underground Electric Railways Company of London for use in dug-outs, huts, etc., in France and other places abroad, Christmas, 1916. The drawing was the gift of the artist

11. L. RAVEN-HILL.

> THE WATCHERS OF THE SEAS. Recruiting poster for the British Navy, 1915.

12. BERNARD PARTRIDGE.

> KOSSOVO DAY IS THE SERBIAN NATIONAL DAY. Poster of a British "Flag Day," June 25, 1916.

13. JOHN HASSALL.

> BELGIAN CANAL BOAT FUND. For relief of the civil population behind the firing lines.

14. JOHN HASSALL.

> MUSIC IN WAR-TIME: GRAND PATRIOTIC CONCERT, ALBERT HALL. Poster of the Professional Classes War Relief Council.

15. BERNARD PARTRIDGE.

> HAVEN. STAR AND GARTER HOME. Poster of the British Women's Hospital Fund, appealing for subscriptions toward the expense of converting the Star and Garter Hotel, Richmond, into a home for men incurably disabled in the War.

16 PAUL NASH.

> Poster of an Exhibition of War Paintings and Drawings at the Leicester Galleries, London, May, 1918.

17. SIR WILLIAM ORPEN, R.A.

> Poster of an Exhibition of War Paintings and Drawings, executed on the Western Front by Major William Orpen. At Agnew's Galleries, London, 1919.

18. NORMAN WILKINSON.

> THE DARDANELLES. WAR SKETCHES IN GALLIPOLI   Poster of an Exhibition at the Fine Art Society, London, 1915.

> (When still compelled to fight and bleed,
> When, suffering deprivation everywhere,
> You go without the coal and warmth you need,
> With ration-cards and darkness for your share
> With peace-time work no longer to be done,—
> Someone guilty there must be—
> England, the Arch-enemy !
> Stand then united, steadfastly !
> For Germany's sure cause will thus be won.)

LIST OF ILLUSTRATIONS

53. KAISER- UND VOLKSBANK FÜR HEER UND FLOTTE. (Kaiser and people's thank-offering for Army and Navy.) Poster for the Frankfort Christmas Offering, 1917.

54. HELFT! DEN BRAVEN SOLDATEN. . . . (Help! for the brave Soldiers. . . . Poster of the Soldiers' Aid Committee, Berlin.

55. ROLAND KRAFTER.
The Troops Home-Coming for Christmas.

56. F. K. ENGELHARD.
ELEND UND UNTERGANG FOLGEN DER ANARCHIE. (Misery and Destruction follow Anarchy.) Poster of the German Revolution, 1918.

57. BIRÓ.
Poster depicting the Russian Invasion.

58. A. K. ARPELLUS.
ZEICHNET 7 KRIEGSANLEIHE. (Subscribe to the Seventh War Loan.)

59. KÜRTHY.
War Loan Poster. Issued in Budapest, 1917.

60. FARAGÓGÉZ.
War Loan Poster. Issued in Budapest.

61. BIRÓ
War Loan Poster. Issued in Budapest, 1917.

62. KÜRTHY
War Loan Poster. Issued in Budapest, 1917.

AMERICAN

63. *RALEIGH.
MUST CHILDREN DIE, AND MOTHERS PLEAD IN VAIN? BUY MORE LIBERTY BONDS.

64. *BOOKS WANTED FOR OUR MEN "IN CAMP AND OVER THERE." Poster of the American Association of Libraries for supplying books to the troops on service.

65. *ELLSWORTH YOUNG.
REMEMBER BELGIUM. BUY BONDS. Poster of the American Fourth Liberty Loan, 1918.

66. ADOLPH TREIDLER.
FOR EVERY FIGHTER A WOMAN WORKER. CARE FOR HER THROUGH THE Y.W.C.A. Poster of the United War Work Campaign, American Y.W.C.A.

CZECHO-SLOVAK

76. *V. PREISSIG

    Czecho-slovaks! Join our Free Colours. One of six posters issued by the Czecho-slovak Recruiting Office, New York, U.S.A. Printed at the Wentworth Institute, Boston, U.S.A.

RUSSIAN

77. Europe and the Idol. How much longer shall we Sacrifice our Sons to this Accursed Idol? (The inscription on the idol is " Anglia.") Revolutionary Poster. ? German propaganda.

GERMAN

78. GIPKINS.

    Bringt euren Goldschmuck den Goldankaufsstellen. (Bring your gold ornaments to the Gold-purchasing Depôt !)

AUSTRIAN

79. ALFRED OFFNER.

    Zeichet 7. Kriegsanlenihe. (Subscribe to the Seventh War Loan.

AMERICAN

80. BABCOCK.

    Join the Navy—the Service for Fighting Men. Recruiting Poster for the U.S. Navy.

I.—POSTERS AND THE WAR

NEVER in the history of the world have the accessories of ordinary civilised life met with so searching a test of their essential quality as during the War. All national effort throughout the belligerent countries was organised and directed to serve a single purpose of supreme importance. This purpose in its turn served as a touchstone to sort out whatever was useful and valuable in everyday things, and shaped the selected elements into weapons of immense power. The poster, hitherto the successful handmaid of commerce, was immediately recognised as a means of national propaganda with unlimited possibilities. Its value as an educative or stimulative influence was more and more appreciated. In the stress of war its function of impressing an idea quickly, vividly, and lastingly, together with the widest publicity, was soon recognised. While humble citizens were still trying to evade a stern age-limit by a jaunty air and juvenile appearance, the poster was mobilised and doing its bit.

Activity in poster production was not confined to Great Britain. France, as in all matters where

Art is concerned, triumphantly took the field, and soon had hoardings covered with posters, many of which will take a lasting place in the history of Art. Germany and Austria, from the very outset of the War, seized upon the poster as the most powerful and speedy method of swaying popular opinion. Even before the War, we had much to learn from the concentrated power, the force of design, the economy of means, which made German posters sing out from a wall like a defiant blare of trumpets. Their posters issued during the War are even more aggressive ; but it is the function of a poster to act as a " mailed fist," and our illustrations will show that, whatever else may be their faults, the posters of Germany have a force and character that make most of our own seem insipid and tame.

Here in Great Britain the earliest days of the War saw available spaces everywhere covered with posters cheap in sentiment, and conveying childish and vulgar appeals to a patriotism already stirred far beyond the conception of the artists who designed them or the authorities responsible for their distribution.* This, perhaps, was inevitable in a country such as ours. The grimness of the world-struggle was not realised in its intensity until driven home

* While this is being written, our authorities are again placarding our walls with indifferent posters showing the advantages of life in the Army as compared with the " disadvantages " of civil life, and embodying an undignified appeal to Britons to join the Army for the sake of playing cricket and football and seeing the world for nothing !

by staggering blows at our very life as a nation. Then, and not till then, a Government which was always halting to " wait and see," or moving slowly behind the nation, at last got into its stride. Artists understood the call and responded. The poster, inspired by an enthusiasm unknown before, became the one form of Art answering to the needs of the moment, an instrument driving home into every mind its emphatic moral and definite message. It is characteristic that the first truly impassioned posters we saw in England were in aid of Belgian refugees or the Belgian Red Cross. They dealt with the violation of Belgium ; and the stirring appeal of the work done by G. Spencer Pryse and Frank Brangwyn, R.A., in those early days will always linger in the memory.

So numerous were the posters issued in every country, both by the Governments concerned and the various committees dealing with relief work and other aspects of the War, that the international collection acquired by the Imperial War Museum exceeds twenty thousand. Large numbers of these, many of them consisting of letterpress only, are outside the scope of the present volume, which is intended to make accessible to the public in a convenient form reproductions of a small selection distinguished for their artistic merit. The collection of original War posters acquired by the Victoria and Albert Museum has provided most of the illustrations. It comprises several hundred posters from Germany, Austria, Hungary, and other countries, in addition to those issued by Great Britain and her Allies; and it illustrates, in a compact form, the finest artistic uses to which colour-lithography was put as a weapon in the World War.

The small collection made for this volume is necessarily arbitrary. Our illustrations are often about one-twelfth the size of the originals, and the limit in size may perhaps be considered to detract from the value of the reproductions. This, however, has been considered, as far as possible, in selecting the examples chosen. A strong, impulsive design does not depend entirely upon size for the force of its appeal, nor does it change in character from being reduced; but a poster badly designed, though passable on a large scale, may be an unintelligible jumble in a small illustration. In many cases a design is knit together by its reduction, and so viewed as a whole more compactly. Its publication in book form gives it also a permanence and ultimately a wider audience than the original can hope to gain.

This thought of the ephemeral character of the poster as such has, in the first instance, prompted the publication of this volume. A poster serving the purposes of a war, even of such a world cataclysm as that during which we have passed during the last five years, is by its nature a creation of the moment, its business being to seize an opportunity as it passes, to force a sentiment into a great passion, to answer an immediate need, or to illuminate an episode which may be forgotten in the tremendous sequence of a few days' events. In its brief existence the poster is battered by the rain or faded by the sun, then pasted over with another message more urgent still. Save for the very limited number of copies that wise collectors have preserved, the actual posters of the Great War will be lost and forgotten in fifty years.

But we must not forget that in every country concerned the poster played its part as an essential munition of war. Look through any collection of them, and you will see portrayed, in picture and in legend, which he who runs may read, the whole history of the Great War in its political and economical aspects. The posters of 1914-1918 illustrate every phase and difficulty and movement— recruiting for naval, military, and air forces; munition works; war loans; hospitals; Red Cross; Y.M.C.A.; Church Army; food economy; land cultivation; women's work of many kinds; prisoners' aid—and hundreds of problems and activities in connection with the country's needs. The same sequence of needs can be traced in the posters of Germany and Austria, where a stress even greater than our own is revealed, not merely in the urgent appeals for contributions to war loans, but in the sale by German women of their jewels and their hair.

For obvious reasons only a limited number of the posters could be reproduced in colour, the main portion of the plates in the book being in black and white. But since the primary element counting for success in the poster is design, it follows that excellent colouring will not save a badly-designed poster from failure, however much it enhances the power of one already successful. Indeed, we may go further and claim that ineffective or quite bad colouring often fails to mar entirely the success of a good design. The examples selected are not heavy losers by being reproduced mostly in monotone; for they are essentially posters depending on design and not merely pictorial advertisements. Their purpose is innate in their structure; they have their story to tell and message to deliver; it is their business to waylay and hold the passer-by, and to impose their meaning upon him. The best of them have done this brilliantly.

II.—GREAT BRITAIN

SHORTLY after the War began, an "Exhibition of German and Austrian Articles typifying Design" was arranged at the Goldsmiths' Hall, to show the directions in which we had lessons to learn from German trade-competitors as to the combination of Art and economy applied to ordinary articles of commerce. The walls were hung with German posters, and one felt at once that while our average poster cost perhaps six times as much to produce, it was inferior to its German rival in just those vital qualities of concentrated design, whether of colour or form, and those powers of seizing attention, which are essential to the very nature of a poster.

While we have had individual poster artists, such as Nicholson, Pryde, and Beardsley, whose work has touched perhaps a higher level than has ever been reached on the Continent, our general conception of what is good and valuable in a poster has been almost entirely wrong. The advertising agent and the business firm rarely get away from the popular idea that a poster must be a picture, and that the purpose of every picture is to " point a moral and adorn a tale." They seldom realise that poster

7

art and pictorial art have essentially different aims. If a British firm wishes to advertise beer, it insists on an artist producing a picture of a publican's brawny and veined arm holding out a pot of beer during closed hours to a policeman ; or a Gargantuan bottle towering above the houses and dense crowds of a market-place ; or a fox-terrier climbing on to a table and wondering what it is "master likes so much"—all in posters produced at great expense with an enormous range of colour. The German, on the other hand—there was an example at the Goldsmiths' Hall—designs a single pot of amber, foaming beer, with the name of the firm in one good spot of lettering below. It is printed at small cost, in two or three flat colours ; but it shouts "beer" at the passer-by. It would make even Mr. Pussyfoot thirsty to glance at it.

Our British love for a story in a picture has accounted for an immense amount of ingenious artistry falling into amorphous ineffectiveness. It is the essence of the poster that it should compel attention ; grip by an instantaneous appeal ; hit out, as it were, with a straight left. It must convey an idea rather than a story. From its very nature it must be simple, not complex, in its methods. If it has something eccentric or bizarre about it, so long as it is good in design, that is a good quality rather than a fault. Even about the best of our war posters one feels that they are too often enlarged drawings, excellent as lithographs to preserve in a collector's portfolio, but ineffective when valued in relation to the essential services that a poster is required to render. We must regretfully admit that when it comes to choosing illustrations for a volume such as this on their merits as posters, not as pictures, it is difficult not to give a totally disproportionate space to posters made in Germany.

Our British war posters are too well known and too recent in our memory to require any lengthy introduction or comment. The first official recognition of their value to the nation was during the recruiting campaign which began towards the close of 1914. The Parliamentary Recruiting Committee gave commissions for more than a hundred posters, of which two and a half million copies were distributed throughout the British Isles. We hope it is not true that, in their wisdom and aloofness, they refused the offer of a free gift of a six-sheet poster by Mr. Frank Brangwyn, R.A. It is, at any rate, certain that they possessed a poor degree of artistic perception, and, added to this, a very low notion of the mentality of the British public. Hardly one of the early posters had the slightest claim to recognition as a product of fine art ; most of them were examples of what any art school would teach should be avoided in crude design and atrocious lettering. Among the best and most efficient, however, may be mentioned Alfred Leete's "Kitchener." But if one compares Leete's head of Kitchener, "Your Country Needs You," with Louis Oppenheim's "Hindenburg," the latter, with its rugged force and reserve of colour, stands as an example of the

2

direction in which Germany tends to beat us in poster art.

While these early official posters perhaps served their purpose—and if they did, it was thanks to the good spirit of the British public and not to the artistic merit of the posters themselves—a series of recruiting posters was issued by the London Electric Railways Company. Even before the War, this Company, or rather their business manager, Mr. F. Pick (for in regard to posters Mr. Pick might well say " L'état, c'est moi "), was setting an example in poster work by securing the services of the best artists of the day. Their recruiting posters were a real contribution to modern art. They served their purpose, and at the same time were dignified in conception, design, and draughtsmanship. Standing high among them in nobility of appeal and power of drawing were Brangwyn's "Britain's Call to Arms," and Spencer Pryse's "Only Road for an Englishman."

Though they were not issued till 1916, we might mention here the series published by the London Electric Railways Company at the time when the restrictions regarding paper prevented the general distribution of posters at home. It was then that the Company thought of the friendly idea of sending to our troops overseas a greeting of the kind so many of them had been familiar with in old days in London. Four posters, to awaken thoughts of pleasant homely things, were sent out for use in dug-outs and huts in France and other places abroad.

Each was headed with the words : "The Under-ground Railways of London, knowing how many of their passengers are now engaged on important business in France and other parts of the world, send out this reminder of home." The drawings were the free gifts of the artists who designed them— George Clausen, R.A., Charles Sims, R.A., F. Ernest Jackson, and J. Walter West. It was a most admirable idea, admirably carried out, and, as were their recruiting posters, a pronounced testimony to the patriotic and disinterested attitude of a great business institution. Everyone who served abroad knows how much these posters were appreciated as a decoration in Army messes, Y.M.C.A. huts, and elsewhere.

To return to the official use of posters, very much better work was produced in 1915 by the Parlia-mentary Recruiting Committee, and also under the auspices of the Ministry of Information, the author-ities having learned at last that, at home, a poster might be a work of art, and that, abroad, an "official artist" might be deemed worthy of a subaltern's rank, rations, and emoluments. Among good posters for which the Government was at this time responsible may be mentioned Bernard Partridge's "Take up the Sword of Justice," Guy Lipscombe's "Our Flag," Doris Hatt's "St. George," Caffyn's "Come along, Boys," and Ravenhill's "The Watchers of the Seas." In this connection it is amus-ing to recall a wireless message circulated from Berlin on October 2, 1915, in which appeared the statement: "To-day the exhibition of all English recruiting posters published up to the present was opened for the benefit of the German Aeronautic Fund. The exhibition is a great material success, notwithstanding the general disappointment at the poor and inartistic designs." It is, of course, an essential part of national propaganda to decry the quality of whatever is produced by the enemy ; but we must admit that in this instance some truth was embodied in the judgment of these hostile critics. It came as a wholesome counterblast to the probably inspired laudatory articles which a little before this date had appeared in our own Press telling us of "several million of forceful and often fine" posters, and that "the hoardings of England have never borne a better message conveyed in a better manner." That many of the posters were comparative failures goes without saying: and there was one real blunder. In connection with the War Savings Campaign the Ministry had the excellent idea of using as a poster Whistler's famous masterpiece—his "Portrait of the Artist's Mother," now in the Louvre. Nothing could have been better: but then they got someone to write across the beautiful background, in paltry lettering, "Old age must come." There could be no better example of our British idea of enforcing a moral. It was an act of vandalism—impossible in France— almost as cruel as the firing of a shell into Rheims Cathedral. And Whistler, who spent hours in considering where he should place his dainty little butterfly signature, must have turned in his grave, or wished that he could have returned to earth to produce a new edition of his " Gentle Art of Making Enemies."

To Mr. G. Spencer Pryse belongs the honour of first realising in actual productions the needs of the time. Mr. Pryse was in Antwerp at the outbreak of war, and thus was an eye-witness of much of the tragedy which overtook Belgium. On the actual scenes of the evacuation were founded his pathetic lithograph of the Belgian refugees struggling into steamers to escape from the advancing terror. Shortly after, he obtained a commission to act as a despatch-rider for the Belgian Government, in which capacity he visited all parts of the front line both in Belgium and in France, and saw a good deal of desultory fighting. Before he was wounded, he drew several of the series of nine lithographs entitled "The Autumn Campaign, 1914," which were published early in 1915. His poster " The Only Road for an Englishman " was of the same period, followed soon afterwards by his powerful pictorial appeal on behalf of the Belgian Red Cross Fund. It is interesting to know that even under the most difficult conditions, and under fire, his drawings were made, not on paper, but on actual lithographic stones carried for the purpose in his motor-car.

The outstanding figure among poster artists, both in quantity and for technical accomplishment, was Mr. Frank Brangwyn, R.A. His " Britain's Call to Arms " was produced in 1914 by the Underground Railways Company, and circulated in large numbers.

The huge lithographic stone upon which this was drawn was subsequently presented, as the joint gift of Sir Charles Cheers Wakefield, Lord Mayor of London, and the artist, to the Victoria and Albert Museum, where it is preserved and exhibited. His invention and activity as a designer of war posters were very considerable. The number of poster designs from his hand produced during the War is at least fifty, without taking into account such additional work as the propaganda lithographs published by the Ministry of Information. Though Mr. Brangwyn's first war poster was prepared in conjunction with the Underground Railways, he was always willing and eager to make designs for any deserving cause, and among the committees he assisted by his vigorous work may be named the 1914 War Society, the Belgian and Allies' Aid League, the National Institute for the Blind, and the *Daily Mail* Red Cross Fund. Practically all these posters were done as a free gift by the artist ; and their number and quality stand as a splendid record of national service. Heaven preserve Mr. Brangwyn from an O.B.E. ! But one wonders whether the Government has no suitable reward for one who spared no effort and sacrificed himself and his time and talent in a purely impersonal desire to serve his country.

III.—FRANCE

BEFORE the Beggarstaff Brothers initiated the reform movement in British poster art—the early phase of which, despite the effective colour sense of Walter Crane, passed away all too soon with the death of Aubrey Beardsley — Chéret, Steinlen, and Mucha were already at work in France, the first and eldest of these masters being practically the creator of the modern poster in its more individual characteristics. A good deal of the Victorian heaviness was still with us in the eighteen-nineties : we liked good solid meals ; our theatres offered us feasts of ponderous sentimentality; and so the British merchant and advertising agent, employing a poster artist, bade him tell us of the things we liked best—sauces, soaps, melodramas, tea, and stout. For still the idea was prevalent that the successful advertiser appealed to his public most when he told them about something they already knew and liked : a sweet domestic scene to linger in the memory after dinner and remind them of Tompkins' pills; or a pleasant landscape executed with a kaleidoscopic richness of colour to persuade one to buy Fishville Sauce. There were, of course, many striking exceptions to this ; but it was generally true enough to justify the American observer's criticism that British posters mostly depicted things to eat, or soap.

But France, being by temperament, by environment, and by tradition a far more artistic nation, with a much higher standard of general taste, responded more readily to the lighter and more fascinating touch of those artists who chose the street and the theatre entrance as their gallery. It is more than fifty years since Chéret started on his flamboyant comet-like career, setting Paris aflame (so to speak) with joyously wild, irresponsible visions of colour and line, delicate and fantastic. Steinlen, Mucha, Grasset, Toulouse - Lautrec, Willette, Bonnard, Guillaume, and others worked with him in more recent days, and among these are artists who have done masterly posters for France during the War.

It is still with the greatest reluctance that a drawing, even when it conveys a definite suggestion clearly, is accepted in England unless it is "finished": the value of a work of art is reckoned in accordance with the amount of patient craftsmanship which it displays. The French poster artist, on the contrary —and he obviously has the public as his supporter, or his vogue would cease—is often content to throw upon the space at his command what, on this side of the Channel, any advertising agent would scoff at and reject as a " mere sketch." If the French artist can convey his suggestion, his idea, in a few hasty lines or brilliant touches of colour, he knows that his work is done, and is well content.

Looking at the French war posters as a whole, one feels that in no other country has there been the same poignant appeal, the same presence of a deeply-felt emotion. And these have been transferred to the posters with a spontaneity, a lightness, and an expressive sufficiency that make the French poster stand alone. Take the posters of Steinlen, Faivre, Willette, Poulbot, and that versatile master, Roll, whose death occurred while these notes were being prepared. They each have the brilliant quality of a sketch by a man who is master of his material. They are drawn with the fine, free gesture of the born narrator. All the balance and compactness of the French *conte* are there, with every line inducing to intensity of expression. In the figures there is nothing of English photographic precision, nothing of Germany's force and brutality, but always a note of intense sympathy, of something subtly human. Rapid, slight, they may be; but there is a greatness and endurance in their design and their appeal. The *poilu*, in the trenches or *en permission*, the *gamin* of the streets, the worker in the field or hospital, the invalid who has been smitten by the heavy blows of war, are alive in these swift chalk-drawn studies.

The whole difference between the British and the French outlook is summed up in Jules Abel Faivre's poster for the *Journée Nationale des Tuberculeux*, with the poignant appeal of the figure in its

3

luminous envelopment of sea and sky. There is no
need for any vandal to write his descriptive note
across the face of this to drive its message home.
The sad tale is told at a glance ; and its brief legend
—"Sauvons-les" (Let us save them)—is not necessary to make the meaning clear, but rather it
delivers an additional message—a note of resolution
and purpose—to the awakened sympathy when the
picture has done its work. Here everything necessary is said : not a superfluous touch to mar its
purpose, nor a touch too little. Yet an English
advertiser would never have been content with those
two comforting hands which pathetically suggest so
much. The suggestion to him would have been
totally inadequate, and he would have insisted on a
full-length nurse in uniform, or a hospital ward, and
medicine bottles, and all sorts of needless detail.

In the earliest months of the War France was
perhaps too heavily shocked by the onslaught, and
too busily engaged in material organisation, to give
much attention to the subject of posters. But
for the *Journée du Poilu* at Christmas-time, 1915
Steinlen, Faivre, Neumon, Poulbot, and Willette
contributed designs which immediately set upon
French war posters the stamp of genuine understanding of the purpose in view and appreciation of
the material at disposal. So, through a long series of
War Loan posters, " Flag-day " appeals, and posters
relating to every phase of life where advertisement
could be a valuable thing till the welcome end was
reached, French artists produced an incomparable

variety of brilliant designs, in which gaiety, pathos, humour, and tragedy were touched with a characteristic lightness of hand, and often touched with true greatness of conception.

Among those who have done the most distinguished work the artists named above have contributed a large proportion. Jules Abel Faivre, whose " Sauvons-les " has already been referred to at length, has perhaps earned more individual fame by his designs than any other French poster artist during the War. Several of his lithographs approach greatness, and two—the " Sauvons-les " and " On les aura !" both of which are illustrated in this book —can be said confidently to attain it. In its way nothing could be better also than Poulbot's sketch of children collecting for the *Journée du Poilu* — " Pour que papa vienne en permission, s'il vous plait." This artist has done several other very excellent posters, showing an intense understanding and appreciation of child life. The humour of Willette, exemplified in the delightful " Enfin seuls . . . !", reproduced here as illustration No. 31, and the dramatic sense of Charles Fouqueray, find ample material for expression, and in their hands it is finely used. Roll, the more complete artist, versatile and subtle in his work, master of many styles, proved that he, too, could design an appealing poster, as the fifth plate in this book testifies.

The poster artists of France were not to the same degree overshadowed by one great executant as were those of England by Brangwyn. But for all that, a figure stands out before the rest, both by his power as a craftsman and the weight and strength of his individual characteristics. Théophile Alexandre Steinlen was at work upon posters twenty-five years ago, and even then he ranked among the first three or four leaders of this branch of art. Like Brangwyn in England, he is a master of the medium he uses— a great lithographer, whose consummate sense of draughtsmanship and design serves him in the expression of noble thought and in portraying the emotions of a profound, large-hearted patriot.

Mention must also be made of the posters by the distinguished Alsatian artist Hansi—a keen patriot, who was willing to spend himself generously in the service of an Alsace longing for freedom from the yoke of Germany. The German Government offered a reward for information that should lead to his arrest, and issued proclamations to that effect, ostensibly on the plea that he had evaded service in their army, but actually because of the pen and brush that in his hands were powerful weapons which they could not afford to despise. His posters depict the fraternisation of French soldiers with the people of Alsace, and one of them the raising of the victorious tricolour once more over the Cathedral of Strasbourg. All honour to the artist, who, in the face of danger, and a fugitive from death, remained the supporter of a cause still far off from victory—a patriot whose work was full of courage and hope for an oppressed people.

HUNGARY.

THOUGH we are dealing in this volume with pictorial posters, it is difficult to refrain from mentioning the poster proclamations issued by the Germans on their occupation of Belgium. Many of these proclamations, of great historical interest, are in the possession of the Imperial War Museum. One of the earliest, posted at Hasselt on August 17, 1914, immediately after the occupation of the town, threatens to kill a third of the male inhabitants should the German troops be fired upon. Another, posted in Andenne on August 21, 1914, states that by order of the German authorities about three hundred inhabitants had been massacred or burnt alive, and that those of the men who were unscathed were taken as hostages and the women made to clear away the pools of blood and remove the corpses.

The most poignant of these poster proclamations are two in regard to the executions of Nurse Cavell and Captain Fryatt. The bill, signed by General von Bissing, October 12, 1915, issued at Brussels and printed in French on blue paper, announces that Nurse Cavell has been shot, with others. Captain

Fryatt had also been shot before the publication of the proclamation relative to him. This document, signed by Admiral von Schröder, dated at Bruges, July 27, 1916, and printed in German, Flemish, and French, in parallel sections, reads :

> " Charles Fryatt, of Southampton, captain in the English Merchant Service, who, although not enrolled in the armed forces of the enemy, attempted on March 28, 1915, to destroy a German submarine by ramming. For this act he was condemned to death by the Naval Council of War and executed. A perverse act thus received its just, if tardy, chastisement."

The only known copy of this poster is in the possession of the French Government, as evidence of German iniquity for which reparation must be exacted. It is worth noting that all these proclamations are rude specimens of typography, a fact indicating the difficulty which the Germans had in getting them printed.

When we pass to the pictorial posters of Germany and Austro-Hungary, we find that the Central Empires, like ourselves and our Allies, found the necessity for a constant stream of posters appealing to their peoples for aid in men and money for the prosecution of the War and for stimulating love of country as expressed in the resolution and determination to hold out to the last. But though the nature of the national appeals are akin, the posters of Germany and Austro-Hungary (we need scarcely continue to distinguish between them) disclose the varying national temperament and idiosyncrasy.

Since the days of Dürer and Holbein, Germany has been barren in pictorial art. In all her applied arts, as well as in her graphic arts, she has followed a policy of skilful adaptation, borrowing and re-moulding on more economic lines the best products of other countries.* On the one hand—in the years before the war—the sanest British methods of typo-graphy and book production were deliberately im-ported into Germany ; on the other hand, the most freakish of cubist and vorticist paintings found in Germany their principal buyers. If any note was added to what she adapted, it was that of an ad-ditional violence—the open assertion of Germany's idea that "force is beauty."

The war posters of Germany act as a mirror to German mentality. They dwell chiefly on one thing—force. Subjects and treatment are often crude and brutal, marked by a scorn and avoidance of human sympathy. Here and there we find a certain sensuous beauty, but, as a rule, they look on life with a coldness that is almost cynicism, an im-passiveness that is nearer cruelty than pity. The remotest student could deduce a clear idea of the

---

* It is worth noting that, after Germany had set a value on Raemaeker's head, her authorities did not disdain to employ his genius, when it suited their purpose, borrowing his famous cartoon "The Dance of Death" for denunciation of Berlin's mad craze for gaiety, with the words "Sein Tanzer ist Tod."

enormous gulf that lies between the national temperament of Germany and of France by a comparison
of the posters of Engelhard, Leonard, and Erler
with those of Steinlen, Faivre, Roll, Poulbot, and
Willette.

But when all that is said, one has to admit that the
German, above all others, does grasp the essential
value of the poster as a means to an end. He realises
that in the best poster there must be something of
what was aimed at in the Post-Impressionist movement in painting, a desire for summarised form,
strong and simplified line, and the reduction of tones
to an arbitrary convention. And though we have
used the word " Post-Impressionism," we are only
suggesting that the poster should accomplish what
the stained-glass window at its best—with a religious
instead of propagandist or commercial purpose—
accomplished five hundred years ago. While the
British poster must see everything in the round,
must try to reproduce all that is intensely obvious in
the varied texture and material pageantry and inex-
haustible colouring of life, Germany is rightly
content to be deliberately abstract, to seek the
common factors from what is large and general, and
to endeavour to find symbols to express ideas. She
is not concerned with the pursuit of spiritual or
physical beauty, but with a striking novelty or
decorative composition. The colour schemes of the
German posters are more curious and insistent than
attractive, but they do possess that knock-down force
which, after all, is the object of a poster. Its pictorial

quality is a secondary matter ; if it is a fine piece of wall decoration that one would like to live with, so much the better ; but its function is to arrest and to make itself remembered. Indeed, the poster must be like a beacon set on a hill to which all eyes must go, all roads must seem inevitably to lead. The beacon is a flare in the night ; the poster must act as a flare in the day.

The famous sentence from the Academy discourses of Sir Joshua Reynolds, which is inscribed as a motto over the entrance to the Victoria and Albert Museum —a sentence much quoted during the Victorian era, but in these latter days perhaps little regarded—may be applied to the poster equally as to more durable and delightful works : " The excellence of every art must consist in the complete accomplishment of its purpose." If the poster which accomplishes its pur- pose is indeed the most " artistic," then Germany excels in the artistic poster. It may be brutal, it may be ugly, it may even shock and repel ; but there is always in the best examples, instinct in their very conception, a definite purpose which gains full ex- pression, because the artist has been trained to limit himself to what he has to say, and to say that with all his might.

The illustrations to this volume include work by several of the German poster artists, which, symp- tomatic of the whole, will serve to illustrate the fore- going remarks. Mention has already been made in the section dealing with British posters of the strong, rugged simplicity of Louis Oppenheim's

4

"Hindenburg." The artist has in this most success-fully imposed upon the spectator, not the bolstered-up individual of real life, but the strong, massive calm we seek for in the ideal leader, the man in whom we can place entire confidence. It is thus, in addition to being a successful poster, a piece of successful propaganda. But as its strength is in its reserve and the quiet it imposes, so in Engelhard you get passion released and surging over the onlooker with its flood of hatred. His "Nein! Niemals!" (illustration No. 43) is a powerful instance of this. It is almost impossible to look at the grasping, claw-like hands and ravenous face without a fury of hate, and a realisation of how Germany mastered her people. "Elend und Untergang folgen der Anarchie" (Misery and Destruction follow Anarchy), a poster of the German Revolution by the same artist, is another example of intense force, but this time, for all the brutality of the bestial gorilla figure, wonderfully held in reserve and simple. Bearing a curious com-parison with the Czecho-Slovak posters by Preissig, published in New York during the last stages of the War, is the German War Loan poster (illustration No. 35, used also as a design for the back of the cover) by Otto Leonard, "Zereisst Englands Macht" (Rend England's Might). Wohlfeld's poster appealing for women's hair, which is reproduced as a frontispiece, and the poster of the Ludendorff Fund for those disabled by the War (illustration No. 46), show other phases of strength and reserve equally good in their way.

The poster used for the front cover of this book is, apart from its own intrinsic merit, a matter of historical interest, insomuch as it served as a figure in the notorious speech to the German National Assembly at Berlin on May 12, 1919, when the peace terms had been handed to the plenipotentiaries at Versailles. Herr Scheidemann in the course of his denunciation of the Allies' terms said :

> "Ladies and Gentlemen,—All over Berlin we see posters which are intended to arouse a practical love for our brothers in captivity ; sad, hopeless faces behind prison bars. That is the proper frontispiece for the so-called Peace Treaty ; that is the true portrait of Germany's future : sixty millions behind barbed wire and prison bars ; sixty millions at hard labour, for whom the enemy will make their own land a prison camp."

The Austrian poster artists, Krafter, Arpellus, and Puchinger, did important work, examples of which are reproduced in this book ; but several of the Hungarian artists, in particular, did distinguished posters, as will be seen by a reference to illustration No. 41, that by Biró, No. 57, and the little group by Biró and Kurtby, Nos. 59, 61, and 62.

V.—UNITED STATES OF AMERICA

IT is a commonplace to say that America is the true home of the advertisement agent; but in considering the history of poster art in the United States, one is surprised to find that so small a proportion of work done in the past shows any striking originality or real grip. In a country whose special capacity has seemed to consist in beating a very large drum repeatedly, often without much provocation, it was to be expected that the very bones and sinews of a poster should be understood, and that results of the highest order should have been obtained. Contrary to this expectation, only a small group of artists doing important work can be named as illustrating the best ability of the revival which, awaking with Chéret, Steinlen, and the others in France, spread to England, and thence normally to America. Of this group, the most able and important exponents of the art were often frankly derivative in their work. Will H. Bradley designed a number of posters which, with those of Penfield, may be said to have brought about the birth of poster art in the United States; but his most successful designs were openly based on the work of Aubrey Beardsley, the originality, charm, and extravagance of whose genius had

28

recently taken the whole art world by storm. And
Edward Penfield, whose pronounced ability seemed
largely directed to the assimilation of different styles,
produced posters excellent in their order, but most
of them obvious work by a devoted and imaginative
disciple of half a dozen schools varying during the
long process of his development. We find him, for
instance, producing an admirable American Steinlen
in 1897, so clearly and frankly in Steinlen's spirit,
yet with such artistic ability and undoubted person-
ality that it could be placed beside the great French
master's work, be identified with it, and yet retain
its own character. This, while excellent in its way,
is of course by no means provocative of a real
national school, but rather serves to cramp the steps
of later exponents of the art, and render their work
lifeless ; and one is not surprised to find that, after
the days of Penfield, Bradley, and Gould, a good
many years passed without any striking development in poster art in America. The last ten years,
however, have discovered artists of pronounced
originality and genius, and the posters of Robert
Wildhack, Adolph Treidler, and Maxfield Parrish—
to mention only three of the most eminent of their
designers of the days immediately before the War—
testified to the existence of a genuine national school,
and led one to expect vital results in the production
of posters inspired by the great world upheaval.

In this, indeed, were the very elements needed to
call out the utmost ability of the national artists.
The United States—we say it with all respect—has a

keener eye for advertisement than any other nation. Let the American loose on a " whirlwind campaign " —whether in aid of church funds, an enormous commercial enterprise, or a world war—and he is in his element. All the possibilities of sign-boards, hoardings, flashlights, and every novelty and contrivance for catching the public eye, have been carried to their farthest limit, either of invention or of human endurance, on the other side of the Atlantic ; and behind all this is the driving power of an intense, restless energy. It is not our place to speak here of the battlefields of Europe, and of how that energy and activity were thrown into the scale to weigh down the balance which had been trembling for so long. But in the United States, as elsewhere, it was inevitable that posters should be among the first munitions of war, and it was to be anticipated that, learning their lesson from the experiences of countries engaged in the struggle whilst their own yet remained in the position of a spectator, the State departments would improve upon the machinery which Europe had produced in this particular cause. To some extent this was done. As regards the magnitude of output, never was there such facility in the production of posters. Immediately on the outbreak of war, the Army, the Navy, and the Treasury Departments plunged into an orgy of advertisement, and employed not only their national artists, but men among the Allies and neutrals who had done distinguished work in the cause of universal freedom. That these artists were not slow to avail themselves of this new field for their restless energies is witnessed by thᵉ work done by Brangwyn and Raemaekers, who, like knights-errant, plunged with enthusiasm into this new campaign. Jonas, too, the French lithographer, was among the artists of other nations employed by the United States, and one of his posters—" Four Years in the Fight "—aiming to provide houses of cheer for the women of France, is reproduced in illustration No. 68.

We cannot, however, too often reiterate the fact that it is not enough to have a pronounced conviction and a definite purpose in doing things of this kind to do them well. The best poster artists—and here again we may instance Steinlen, Brangwyn and Pryse —are generally craftsmen of the highest order, having a very true sense of the historical development, and a perfect acquaintance with the mechanism and technique, of their art. This knowledge counts enormously, and is visible in the whole structure of the work produced. The bureaucrat who sits in his office conducting a hurried campaign on the telephone, and patronising art when at length it proves necessary to the community, fails on account of his ignorance of the real roots of the matter. The nation needed posters, so the American bureaucrat, like his brother in Whitehall, issued orders for posters to be designed —in much the same way as the British Food Controller ordered bacon to be provided, without a staff of provision experts to see that it was first properly cured.

It is, perhaps, a pity that Mr. Joseph Pennell's

book on his own Liberty Loan poster* was not written as a textbook for the use of Government Departments earlier in the day. The writing of an elaborate treatise on a single war poster may seem at first sight to be giving altogether disproportionate importance even to an admirable example of this type of art, and it is in danger of placing the exponent under the accusation of appreciating his own labours at an excessively high value. But when all things like this have been said, the fact remains that the volume is a serious and dignified exposition of a fine poster by a craftsman who considers that due weight should be given to all that pertains to its actual production, from the original conception of the design to the satisfactory register and inking of the final stone. It should act as a wholesome corrective of the usual slipshod treatment accorded to the artist. Mr. Pennell is at least an enthusiastic lithographer. He knows the business right through; and his little series of essays should leave his reader convinced that a poster grows in power and influence upon the spectator just in accordance with the genuine craftsmanship displayed in it.

The total effect of a poster is cumulative: we feel its design; but we feel its design more strongly for its fitting colour scheme; and still more strongly when the designer knows and works upon all the subtle qualities and texture of the stone he uses.

* Joseph Pennell's " Liberty Loan Poster." A textbook for artists and amateurs, Governments and teachers and printers. 1918.

For its maximum influence the poster must be designed by a skilled lithographic artist (if lithography should be the medium chosen), executed upon stone by him, and printed either by him or under his direct supervision. It is the failure to appreciate this which has marred so many of the United States posters, and made them of little importance. Anyone who could draw has been considered suitable for the task of designing ; anyone who could print has been considered equal to printing their posters. And so we have a great mass of work, some lithographed, some photo-lithographed, some produced from photo-process blocks in colour on varieties of glazed, unsuitable papers ; but very few which leave one with the cool, satisfied feeling that here is good work well done. The influence of a work of art is an elusive thing, easily lost ; and to a full understanding of it years of special training are necessary. The passer in the street may be unaware of the causes of his admiration or sympathy, but the effects upon him have been proved times without number.

Necessarily, however, there are many exceptions to this general failure in craftsmanship, cases in which artists triumphed over all mechanical obstacles, and instances of great lithographic firms, with contracts from the Government, who were skilled in poster production and able to act in genuine consonance with the designers. If we set up a well-defined standard, and place in the front rank men like Raleigh, Treidler, Pennell, and Young, who are

5

very able lithographic artists, producing posters of a high order, there still remains a large group of designers whose work may be characterised as possessing, in a pronounced degree, what has been described as the "poster sense." They may not have the craftsmanship to make the poster all that—viewed as a complete artistic production—it should be; but there is "punch" in their sure and speedy way of conveying a message, in the pithiness and wit of their legends. Above all, they possess a great humanity—that sense of human suffering to be relieved, human wrongs to be righted, which kept the United States a beneficent neutral so long, and at length called her into the War. This is exemplified in their very best work. Raleigh's "Must Children Die, and Mothers Plead in Vain?" reproduced in No. 63, nobly illustrates it. Several other fine posters by this artist, in a style perhaps reminiscent of Brangwyn, yet full of original energy and stirred by genuine passion, deal with the same or similar sentiments. A large number of posters of varying merit follow this lead: "America the Home of All who Suffer, the Dread of All who Wrong," runs the legend on a poster by Paus; "Remember Belgium—Buy Bonds," says another; and it is a general strain.

The recruiting posters in particular have a freedom of design, a vigour and grip, which really tell. For when America came into the War, she started to hustle with all the feverish pent-up energy characteristic of the race. Posters like Christy's pretty girl in naval uniform exclaiming, "Gee! I wish I were a Man.   I'd join the Navy"; Bancroft's ringing " To Arms !" and Whitehead's "Come on !" show a vigour and freshness which our official British recruiting posters never possessed.   There was an air of glad youth in them which came like a Spring wind over our war-weary spirits.

In America, as elsewhere, all forms of activity were announced by posters — Recruiting, Food Economy, Red Cross Work, Homes for Women in France, War Loans, the organising of Polish and Czecho-Slovak citizens,* all kinds of propaganda, were advertised by this means.

It is unnecessary to draw further attention to Mr. Pennell's poster, " That Liberty shall not Perish from the Earth."   He states his own intention in designing it: "My idea was New York City bombed, shot down, burning, blown up by an enemy, and this idea I have tried to carry out."   He conveys, in an effective colour scheme, the impression of a purely imaginary air-raid—a raid that never was on sea or land—with results highly picturesque and impossible.   It is to be reckoned, however, as one of the successful posters of the War.

Adolph Treidler in several designs has justified the expectations founded on his pre-war work, as will be seen from one of his posters here reproduced (illustration No. 66).   The work of Young and Morgan is worthy of the highest commendation ; and for Raleigh's steady craftsmanship and noble designs there can be nothing but praise.

* The Czecho-Slovak posters are referred to in the following chapter.

VI.—OTHER COUNTRIES

TO make a comprehensive survey of posters related to the War in all countries where they were issued would be a formidable task, not so much on account of the quantity of work of outstanding artistic merit, but because the range and variety of mediocre posters, which probably answered their purpose with tolerable efficiency at the moment, is so very extensive. All the nations engaged in the combat had something to proclaim in this manner, often a message of life or death, and others had much to display in propaganda posters all over the world.

Of the chief belligerents not yet mentioned, it is notable that Italy, the native home of the arts, produced few posters of the ordinary type that possessed either originality or definite individual character. The journalistic cartoon, always a powerful means of propaganda in Italy, had a great vogue in the earliest months of the war; and the most popular and able artists of the country fought for the Allied cause with an abandon and self-denial that one remembers with the warmest gratitude. In June and July, 1916, an exhibition of drawings was held at the Leicester Galleries, entitled " Italian Artists and the War." There were several actual poster designs, but by far the larger proportion of the drawings exhibited consisted of war cartoons and caricatures akin to those of Raemaekers and Dyson, though prints from them were extensively displayed upon newspaper bills and walls in Rome and other Italian cities. Serving a double purpose, they were to this extent small posters, and cannot be dismissed without some word of the high praise due to them. Such an incessant and effective war was waged upon Germany and German ideals by these cartoons that, before Italy threw in her lot with the Allies, the Embassies of the Central Powers sought to stay their issue, and to that end prosecuted the most prolific and merciless of the cartoonists, Gabriele Galantara. Cynicism, scorn, contempt, and an utter abhorrence of Germany and all her acts are expressed in these impulsive sketches ; and it is no wonder that they acted as a powerful spur upon the Italian people, showing which way led towards freedom and humanity. It would seem, however, that this great campaign, begun so early by the Italian artists before their nation was ready to participate in the struggle, and continued with a violent energy during the earliest months of Italian fighting, exhausted their resources to a considerable extent. Moreover, many of the most eminent among them—Sachetti, Oppo, Ventura, Codognato, and others—at once joined the Italian forces, mostly as combatants, and a few older men, like Pogliaghi, accompanied the armies to illustrate, in thrilling terms, the formidable achievements of their country amid the mighty fastnesses of the Tyrol. When the time arrived for the Italian Government to issue War Loan and other posters, the most capable of her designers were no longer accessible.

The experience of other nations shows that really noble posters have been produced through artists being inspired by the cause rather than as a result of their employment by the State. Italy proved no exception to this. Such of her best designers as were left still devoted their energies to the production of cartoons; and in due time others returned to their previous work, wounded, like Oppo, cartoonist of the *Idea Nationale*, who, when the 130th Infantry Regiment was annihilated in July, 1915, was one of the five survivors, and came back to his paper with a useless arm, to wage war as of old for land and liberty. The cartoon being thus the most natural means of propaganda in Italy, such posters of the ordinary type as were produced were, in consequence, of an extremely secondary order; so much so that, in making a selection to exhibit at the Grafton Galleries in June, 1919, the Imperial War Museum chose only eight to represent Italy, and of the eight three were posters advertising Raemaekers' cartoons. One of these, "Neutral America and the Hun," is reproduced in illustration 75. Among the actual Italian examples, Barchi's "Sotto-scrivete" and Mauzan's "Fate tutti il vostro dovere" alone were notable.

Greece, on the contrary, showed a considerable

facility in the production of war posters. But anxious as one is to consider in a favourable light whatever artistic creation emanates from the land which inspired and nourished Western art in its infancy, it is impossible to regard their war posters with anything more than an indulgent eye. Mr. Pennell, in his little book to which we have already referred, has claimed all notable productions in decorative art through the ages as posters, and would bid us look on the frieze of the Parthenon as an excellent piece of Greek poster art. It is a wild application, not to be taken too seriously. Modern art is not necessarily a development from the art of other ages ; and even where the form is comparable, the purpose is widely divergent. For a vital modern art is for ever the expression of a new spirit, the revelation of a fresh aspect of life, another facet of a many-sided jewel ; and it is this unexpected quality, the surprise of this revelation, which is so valuable to the world. Nothing new, nothing fresh, appeared in the Greek posters : tame and poor in line, meagre in their quality as reproductions, we must regard them as a brave attempt rather than applaud their achievement.

Japanese posters issued during the War attracted some attention, and favourable comment has been made from time to time upon their merits ; but it seems probable that the quaint English inscriptions many of them bore, rather than their intrinsic qualities as posters, beguiled the critics into taking a genial and generous view of their worth. Such sentences as "The severe battle at the Kuragaw—German troops are extremely defeated," "Our troops attack on Tsingan Retreat German Army and Affrighted," and a very happy mis-spelling, "The Gritish *Sydney* forced the German *Emden* to fight and the sharp action that ensued," are naturally attractive and amusing. The Japanese, in their colour-printing from wood blocks, invented the most perfect poster technique in the world for use on a small scale. The theatrical posters they produced in the eighteenth and early nineteenth centuries could not be surpassed. They contain in miniature all the qualities we most value in this branch of art, and are at the present day as fresh and enthralling as if they referred to matters of contempr.ary interest. The Japanese have proved themselves a wonderfully adaptable race: they have utilised our modern engines of war with an amazing application, and avoided errors, not always obvious, into which other nations have fallen. But while this has its admirable side in the mechanical things of life, imitation in the processes of art proves altogether a failure. The cld Japanese spirit has departed. One is tempted to think that the Japanese understanding of their native art is on the wane. For their posters very little can be said. The curse of European influence is apparent in the modern cheap lithographs, crude in colour and design, which they have produced. We have not been fortunate in finding one that would worthily serve the purpose of an illustration.

Of the British Colonies, Australia, Canada, and

South Africa produced posters of quite a high standard. The eminence attained by the artists of the *Sydney Bulletin* led one to expect some notable examples from New South Wales ; but that province, noble as its achievements were through the fighting qualities of its sons, contributed little to poster art. The Canadian poster reproduced in illustration 74, simple in idea and design, with its fitting legend, shows what promise there is, and indeed attainment, among the Western children of our race. A poster from India (illustration No. 72) is interesting, since it makes an appeal to the Marathas in their own tongue, and in what we are given to understand is tolerably good native verse. The designer, however, is an Englishman resident in India.

A few Russian posters made their appearance previous to the Revolution in that unhappy country. Others have occasionally been issued since, though we have seen none of any outstanding merit. We reproduce, in illustration No. 77, a poster which, when exhibited, was described as a " Bolshevist cartoon " ; but there seems more reason to regard it as an example of German propaganda in Russia, of the period following the so-called Peace of Brest-Litovsk. Europe, a sad and worn woman, stands with a youth before an idol which bears the name " Anglia " ; below is the inscription, in Russian characters: "How much longer shall we sacrifice our sons to this accursed idol?" It is at best a poor thing, and, if German, most carefully designed to bear the impress of a Russian product.

6

A series of six eminently successful posters was issued as an appeal to the Czecho-Slovak people in the United States. For consistent merit, alike in design, colour, and general conception, they take a high place among the posters of the War. The artist, V. Preissig, is a Bohemian living in America, who did the work for the sake of recruiting his fellow-countrymen there. Perhaps the best of them is that shown in our coloured illustration, No. 76, "Czecho-Slovaks! Join our free colours!" with its flags of the four Bohemian States as its main feature, carried by marching men whose heads come in dark silhouette along the bottom of the design. The poster is admirably planned, and the lettering on this and the whole series is simple and distinguished.

Many of us in England recall with amusement the various spy stories which went the rounds among otherwise perfectly reliable people in the early days of the War. We all seemed for a time to have an intimate friend or relation whose nursery governess, butler, or confidential clerk had been discovered in a wanton act of espionage. It was on the most un-impeachable authority. Happily it was left for Brazil to embody its attack of this spy-fever in the form of a poster. "Keep your eyes open and your mouth shut," runs its legend. The poster shows representations of the different disguises under which spies are probably concealing themselves—as nurse-maids, schoolboys, tramps, and so on—and warns the public to avoid them. Life in Brazil would doubtless be exciting for an innocent stranger whilst the mania lasted.

Holland, living in dangerous proximity to our principal enemy, sought generally to avoid material of an inflammatory nature in her posters. Very few of them are notable. We illustrate in colour, on Plate 73, the poster of an exhibition at Tilburg of the " Fraternelle Belge," one of the most satisfactory examples of this class produced in the country. Such institutions as this and the Dutch Anti-War Society are typical sources of inspiration for their posters during the War. But a word must be said of the one exception, the Dutch artist whose force of character and definiteness of aim made him, though a neutral, a protagonist in the cause for which our country's blood was being shed. Louis Raemaekers, cartoonist of the Amsterdam *Telegraaf*, fearless knight-errant for the sake of humanity, who toiled with a pencil of flame against the outragers and oppressors of prostrate Belgium, was worth an invincible battalion to the Allies. His posters were few, and not usually issued in Holland. It is by his cartoons that he will be remembered, a great universal figure, with an irresistible passion for freedom which found full expression in his numberless masterly drawings.

INDEX TO ARTISTS' NAMES

NOTE.—*The heavy black numerals indicate pictures in the book ; the* number of the picture *is given in this case.*

45

PRINTED IN GREAT BRITAIN BY BILLING AND SONS, LTD., GUILDFORD

REPRODUCTIONS OF POSTERS
GROUPED UNDER THE COUNTRIES OF ISSUE

2.

BERNARD PARTRIDGE.

"Take up the Sword of Justice."

Issued by the Parliamentary Recruiting Committee:
No. 106 of their posters.

TAKE UP THE
SWORD OF JUSTICE

3.

F. ERNEST JACKSON.

"Song to the Evening Star."

This poster was one of a group of four which were sent out by the Underground Electric Railways Company of London for use in dug-outs, etc., in France and other places abroad, Christmas, 1916   The drawing was the gift of the artist.

Star that bringest home the bee,
And sett'st the weary labourer free!
If any star shed peace, 'tis Thou
That send'st it from above,
Appearing when Heaven's breath & brow
Are sweet as hers we love.

Come to the luxuriant skies,
Whilst the landscape's odours rise,
Whilst far off lowing herds are heard
And songs when toil is done,
From cottages whose smoke unstirr'd
Curls yellow in the sun.

Star of love's soft interviews
Parted lovers on thee muse,
Their remembrancer in Heaven
Of thrilling vows thou art,
Too delicious to be riven
By absence from the heart.

'Song to the Evening Star.' Thomas Campbell

4.

T. GREGORY BROWN.
"Their Home, Belgium, 1918"
British War Loan poster.

THEIR HOME !

BELGIUM 1918

BUY
National War Bonds
and protect YOUR HOME

5.

FRANK BRANGWYN, R A.

"Britain's Call to Arms."

Recruiting poster, published by the Underground Electric Railways Company of London, 1914.   The stone upon which Mr. Brangwyn drew this lithograph—the first great poster of the War—was subsequently presented to the Victoria and Albert Museum

6.

J. WALTER WEST.

" Harvest-Time, 1916 · Women's Work on the Land "
Issued by the Underground Electric Railways Company
of London.

FRANK BRANGWYN, R A.

Poster for the French Army Orphanage.

" To ensure that the little orphans shall have a home and
motherly care, education in the country, a career suited
to each child, and the religion of their fathers "

ORPHELINAT
DES ARMÉES

ASSURER AUX PETITS ORPHELINS::
LE FOYER ET LA TENDRESSE MATERNELLE
L'ÉDUCATION AU PAYS. UNE CARRIÈRE
APPROPRIÉE A CHAQUE ENFANT. LA
RELIGION DE LEURS PÈRES

8.

GERALD SPENCER PRYSE.

"THE ONLY ROAD FOR AN ENGLISHMAN. THROUGH DARKNESS TO LIGHT; THROUGH FIGHTING TO TRIUMPH."

Published by the Underground Railways Company of London, Ltd., 1914.

9.

GERALD SPENCER PRYSE.

"BELGIUM REFUGEES IN ENGLAND."

Poster of the Belgian Red Cross Fund in London, 1915.

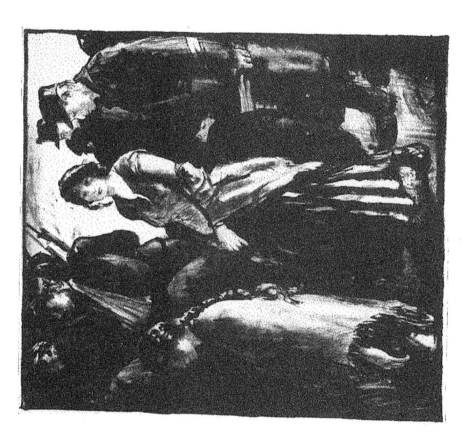

10.

GEORGE CLAUSEN, R.A.

"MINE BE A COT BESIDE THE IIILL"

This poster was one of a group of four which were sent out by the Underground Electric Railways Company of London, for use in dug-outs, huts, etc., in France and o her places abroad, Christmas, 1916. The drawing was the gift of the artist.

11.

L. RAVEN-IIILL.

"THE WATCHERS OF THE SEAS."

Recruiting poster for the British Navy, 1915.

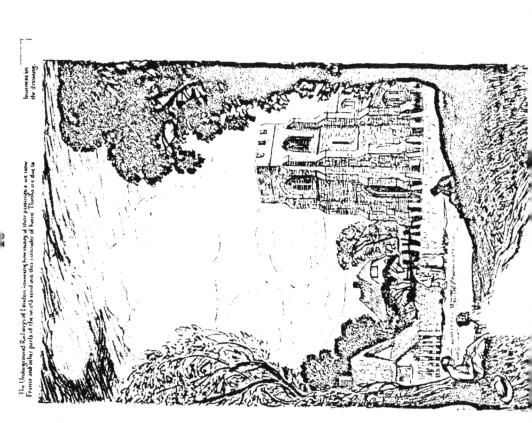

THE WATCHERS OF THE SEAS.

THE NAVY NEEDS BOYS AND MEN FROM

The Underground Railways of London showing how many of their passages are now France and other parts of the world stand out this remainder of home. Thumbs are due to business in the drawing.

BERNARD PARTRIDGE.

1389-1916 .

"Kossovo Day is the Serbian
National Day"

Poster of a British "Flag Day." 25th
June, 1916.

Pos

14.

JOHN HASSALL

"Music in War-Time."

Grand Patriotic Concert, Albert Hall.

Poster of the Professional Classes War
Relief Council.

Poste
Fund
the

1389 **KOSSOVO DAY** **1916**

IS THE

SERBIAN NATIONAL DAY

HEROIC SERBIA.

AT the Battle of Kossovo in 1389, Christianity and Freedom were over-
whelmed in the Balkans, but the Serbs have each year since then kept the
day in stern determination to be free once more. They drove back the
Turks, they twice drove back the Austrians. To-day, Serbia, exiled but not
disheartened, asks us to join in the celebration of her National Day, as a
pledge of the Allies' Victory and Anglo-Serbian Friendship.

KOSSOVO DAY COMMITTEE, 90 PARLIAMENT STREET, S.W.

Belgian Canal Boat Fund

Send Them Something

MUSIC IN WAR-TIME

GRAND Patriotic CONCERT

ROYAL ALBERT HALL
Saturday
April 24th
3 p.m.

PROFESSIONAL CLASSES WAR RELIEF COUNCIL.

STAR & GARTER HOME

TOTALLY DISABLED SOLDIERS AND SAILORS

Haven

You can never repay these utterly broken men. But you
can show your gratitude by helping to build this Home where
they will be tenderly cared for during the rest of their lives.
LET EVERY WOMAN SEND WHAT SHE CAN TO-DAY
to the Lady Cowdray Hon Treasurer The British Women's
Hospital Fund 21 Old Bond Street W

16.

PAUL NASH.

Poster of an Exhibition of War Paintings
and Drawings by Paul Nash at the
Leicester Galleries, London, May, 1916.

18.

NORMAN WILKINSON.

"THE DARDANELLES."
War Sketches in Gallipoli
Poster of an Exhibition at the Fine Art
Society, London, 1915

PAUL NASH
AN OFFICIAL ARTIST ON THE WESTERN FRONT

WAR PAINTINGS & DRAWINGS
LEICESTER GALLERIES
LEICESTER SQ WC2
10 TILL 6 ADMISSION 1/3 INCLUDING TAX

17

WAR
PAINTINGS & DRAWINGS
EXECUTED ON THE WESTERN FRONT BY
MAJOR WILLIAM
ORPEN

EXHIBITION
UNDER THE DIRECTION OF THE
MINISTRY OF INFORMATION
AT
MESSRS AGNEW'S GALLERIES
43 OLD BOND STREET PICCADILLY W
ADMISSION 1/ OPEN 10 TO 6

THE DARDANELLES
WAR SKETCHES IN GALLIPOLI
BY NORMAN WILKINSON R.I.

THE FINE ART SOCIETY
148 NEW BOND ST.

AT
NEUVE CHAPELLE

YOUR FRIENDS NEED
YOU, BE A MAN

20.

POULBOT

" POUR QUE PAPA VIENNE EN PERMISSION, S'IL VOUS PLAIT "
(So that papa may come on leave, if you please)

Poster of the French " Flag Days" in Paris, 25th and
26th December, 1915.

Pour que papa vienne en permission, s'il vous plaît.

21.

AUGUSTE ROLL.

" Pour les Blessés de la Tuberculose."
(For those wounded by tuberculosis)

Poster of the National Day for the Benefit of ex-Soldiers
suffering from Tuberculosis   Paris, 1916

D. CHARLES FOUQUERAY

"Le Cardinal Merciér protége la Belgique."
(Cardinal Mercier protects Belgium)

Poster published in Paris, 1916.

23.

JULES ABLE FAIVRE.

"On les aura!" (We shall get them!)
Subscribe.

Poster of the Second National Defence Loan.

24.

JULES ABEL FALVRE

" Sauvons-les ! " (Let us save them !)

Poster of the National Day for the benefit of ex-Soldiers
suffering from tuberculosis.

JOURNÉE NATIONALE DES TUBERCULEUX
ANCIENS MILITAIRES

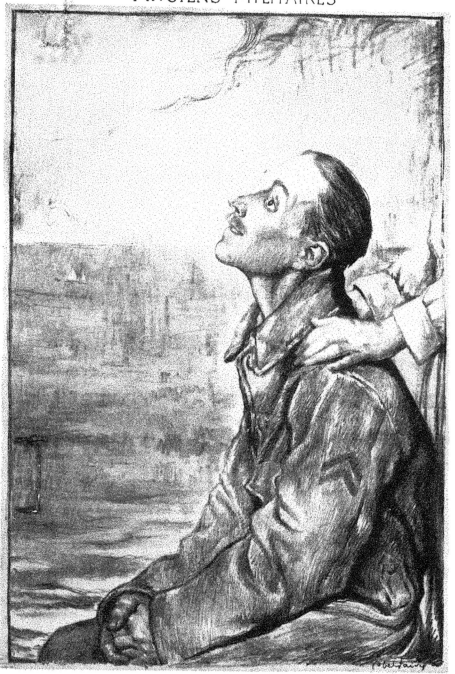

Sauvons-les

25.

D. CHARLES FOUQUERAY.

" La Journée Serbe, 25 Juin, 1916."

Poster of a French " Flag Day " for the Serbian Relief
Fund, on the Anniversary of the Battle of Kossovo.

A JOURNÉE SERBE
25 JUIN 1916
NNIVERSAIRE DE LA BATAILLE DE KOSSOVO

26.

G. CAPON

"La Femme Française pendant la Guerre"
(French Women during the War.)

Poster of the Kinematograph Section of the French Army.

LA FEMME FRANÇAISE PENDANT LA GUERRE

SECTION CINEMATOGRAPHIQUE de l ARMEE FRANÇAISE

27.

SEM.

" Pour le dernier quart d'heure . . . aidez-moi ! "
(For the last quarter of the hour . . . help me !)

Poster of the French War Loan, 1918.

pour le dernier quart d'heure...

aidez-moi!...

ES SOUSCRIPTIONS A L'EMPRUNT NATIONAL SONT REÇUES A LA

BANQUE NATIONALE DE CRÉDIT

LAMBEZ, IMP. PARIS

VISA N° 13-02

28.

THÉOPHILE ALEXANDRE STEINLEN.

ter of the French "Flag Days," 25th and 26th December, 1915   Organized by Parliament.

29.

MAURICE NEUMON.

Poster of the French "Flag Days," 25th and December, 1915   Organized by Parliament.

25 ET 26
DÉCEMBRE
1915

ORGANISÉE PAR LE PARLEME

25 ET 26
DÉCEMBRE
1915

ORGANISÉE PAR LE PARLEMENT

30.

JULES ABEL FAIVRE.

"Pour out your Gold for France.
Gold fights for Victory."

Poster of the French War Loan, 1915.

31.

ADOLPHE WILLETTE.

" By Ourselves at last !"

Poster of the French "Flag Days," 25th and 26th
December, 1916   Organized by Parliament.

Enfin seuls...!

ORGANISÉE PAR LE PARLEMENT

25 ET 26 DÉCEMBRE 1915

DEVAMBEZ Imp. PARIS

LIBERTÉ · ÉGALITÉ · FRATERNITÉ

1915

L'Or Combat Pour La Victoire

32.

JULES ADLER.

"They, too, are doing their Duty."

Poster of the French War Loan, 1915.

33.

AUGUSTE LEROUX

"Subscribe for France who is Fighting! and for that Little One who grows bigger every Day."

Poster of the third French War Loan.

Souscrivez

—AUGUSTE LEROUX

pour la France qui combat !
pour Celle qui chaque jour grandit.

34.

PLONTKE.

"Für die Kriegsanleihe!"
(For the War Loan.)

German War Loan poster issued in Berlin.

Für die
Kriegsanleihe!

W·Hagelberg·Akt·Gef·Berlin·NW 6

35.

OTTO LEHMANN

"Sтutzt unsre Feldgrauen. Zerreisst Englands Macht.
Zeichnet Kriegsanleihe"
(Support our Field Greys. Rend England's might. Sub-
scribe to the War Loan)

Issued in Cologne

36.

ERWIN PUCHINGER.

' ZEICHNET 5½% DRITTE KRIEGSANLEIHE."
(Subscribe to the 5½% Third War Loan.)

Issued in Vienna.

ZEICHNET

5½% dritte KRIEGS-ANLEIHE

37.

ERLER.

" DER 9TE PFEIL.   ZEICHNET KRIEGSANLEIHE "
(The ninth arrow   Subscribe to the War Loan.)

German War Loan poster.

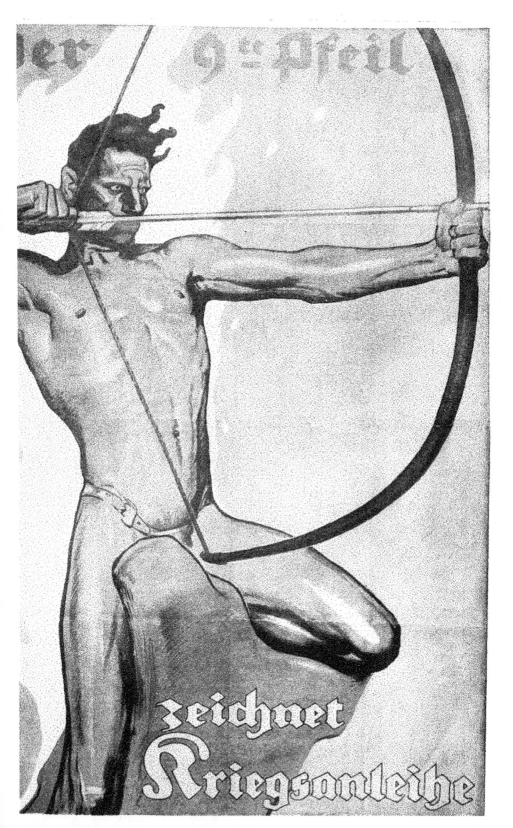

LEONARD.

"DER HAUPTFEIND IS ENGLAND."

"When, still compelled to fight and bleed,
When, suffering deprivation everywhere,
You go without the coal and warmth you need,
With ration-cards and darkness for your share,
With peace-time work no longer to be done,—
Someone guilty there must be—
England, the arch-enemy !
Stand then united, steadfastly !
For Germany's sure cause will thus be won."

39.

H R ERDT

"SOLL UND HABEN DES KRIEGS-JAHRES 1917"
(Losses and gains of the War year 1917.)

German propaganda poster.

40.

OSWALD POLTE.

"Dem Vaterlande!"
"Pommersche Juwelen und Goldankaufswoche
30 Juni—6 Juli."
(For the Fatherland)

Poster advertising the "Pommeranian sale veek for
jevels aid gold, 30 Juie—6th July."

Issued in Berlin.

Dem Vaterlande!

Oswald Polte

Pommersche Juwelen- u. Goldankaufswoche

30. Juni — 6. Juli

41.

A. S.

"Zeichnet funfte Österreichische Kriegsanleihe."
(Subscribe to the fifth Austrian War Loan.)

Poster issued in Vienna.

ZEICHNET FÜNFTE
ÖSTERREICHISCHE
KRIEGSANLEIHE
K·K·PR·
OESTERREICHISCHE
LÆNDERBANK

GYEZZÜNK
IKÖLCSÖNT

43.

F. K. ENGELHARD.

"Nein! Niemals!" (No! Never!)

German poster.

44.

GERD PAUL.

"Es gilt die letzen Schläge,
den Sieg zu vollenden!
Zeichnet Kriegsanleihe!"

(It takes the last blow to make victory complete.
Subscribe to the War Loan!)

45.

M. LENZ.

"Zeichnet achte Kriegsanleihe."
(Subscribe to the eighth War Loan.)

Austrian poster, issued in Vienna.

46.

OLAF GULBRANSSON

Poster of the Ludendorff Fund for the Disabled
Published 1918.

ZEICHNET ACHTE
KRIEGSANLEIHE

Ludendorff-Spende für Kriegsbeschädigte

47.

SPOSIZIONE DE GUERRA, TRIESTE, 1917."
(War Exhibition, Trieste, 1917)

Austrian poster

48

" ZEICHNET VIERTE ÖSTERREICHIS•
KRIEGSANLEIHE."
(Subscribe to the fourth Austrian
Loan.)

49.

" ÖSTERR-UNGAR, KRIEGSGRABER
AUSSTELLUNG "
(Austrian-Hungarian War Graves
Exhibition)

Poster of an Exhibition in Berlin

50.

DANKÓ.

"BE A VOROS HADSEREGBE ! "
(For the conquering army !)

Hungarian War Loan poster.

(1st Communism . 1919.

FBANKE.

"Willst Du den Frieden ernten
Musst Du säen—darum."
(If you vould reap peace,
You must sov to that end)

Postor of the eighth Austrian War Loan

" Kaiser- und Volksdank für Heer und
Flotte."
Kaiser and people's thanksoffering for
Army and Navy)

Poster for the Frankfort Christmas
offering, 1917.

Willst Du den Frieden ernten
Musst Du säen ——— darum

Zeichne 8. KRIEGSANLEIHE bei der
k.k. priv. Bank & Wechselstuben-
Actien-Gesellschaft. MERCUR

Annahmestelle
und Sammelbeutelausgabe:
Schüler-Sammeldienst
der Stadt Mainz
Mainstraße 36

Kaiser-u. Volksdank
für Heer und Flotte

Frankfurter
Weihnachtsgabe
1917

Geldspenden:
Theaterplatz 14, Büro 5

helft!

Den braven Soldaten, die auf der Rückfahrt nach
der Heimat nach schwerer Not Berlin passieren,
muß Unterstützung werden. Überweist der
Soldatenrathilfe
Geld — die Kommandantur von Berlin schafft
damit den Bedürftigen Hilfe!
Eile tut not!

55.

ROLAND KRAFTER.

The troops home-coming for Christmas.

Austrian poster.

57.

BIRÓ.

Hungarian poster depicting the Russian
invasion.

Issued in Budapest.

59.

KÜRTHY.

Hungarian War Loan poster.

Issued in Budapest, 1917.

61.

BIRÓ.

Hungarian War Loan poster.

Issued in Budapest, 1917

61

62

63

RALEIGH.

"Must Children Die and Mother plead in Vain?
Buy more Liberty Bonds."

American War Loan poster.

MUST CHILDREN DIE AND MOTHERS PLEAD IN VAIN ?

Buy More
LIBERTY BONDS

64.

"Books wanted for our Men in Camp and 'Over There'"
Poster of the American Association of Libraries for
supplying books to the troops on service.

65.

ELLSWORTH YOUNG.

"Remember Belgium."

"Buy Bonds Fourth Liberty Loan."

American poster, 1918

66.

ADOLPH TREIDLER.

"For every fighter a woman worker,
Care for her through the Y.W.C.A"

Poster of the United War Work Campaign, American Y.W.C.A.

For
EVERY
FIGHTER
a
WOMAN
WORKER

UNITED
WAR
WORK
CAMPAIGN

CARE
for
HER

through The YWCA

67.

JOSEPH PENNELL.

"THAT LIBERTY SHALL NOT PERISH FROM THE EARTH."

Poster of the fourth American War Loan, 1918.

68.

L. JONAS.

"FOUR YEARS IN THE FIGHT—
THE WOMEN OF FRANCE.
WE OWE THEM HOUSES OF CHEER."

American poster.

The Women of France
We Owe Them Houses of Che

UNITED WAR WORK CAMPAIGN

THAT LIBERTY SHALL NOT
PERISH FROM THE EARTH
BUY LIBERTY BONDS
FOURTH LIBERTY LOAN

American Food Economy poster.

69.

"AMERICA CALLS.
ENLIST IN THE NAVY."
Recruiting poster for the U.S. Navy, 1917.

LOUIS RAEMAEKERS.

"ENLIST IN THE NAVY."

"AMERICANS! STAND BY UNCLE SAM FOR
LIBERTY AGAINST TYRANNY."
—THEODORE ROOSEVELT.

Recruiting poster for the U.S. Navy.

71.

72.

CECIL L. BURNS.

"VICTORY TO THE MARATHAS!"

"Unite, ye men,
And from his strongholds drive the foe,
Nothing but deeds like these can win
A fame that shall endure."

Anglo-Indian recruiting poster. Issued in Bombay, 1915.

72

71

69

73.

A. O.

" In Belgie by De Zorg."
(The home ot distiess in Belgium.)

" Belgian Art for Belgian Distress."

Poster of an Exhibition at Tilburg, Holland, 1917.
La Fraternelle Belge.

BELGISCHE KUNST voor BELGISCHE ZORGEN
DRUK. KOTTING AMSTERDAM
1915 TILBURG 1917
LA FRATERNELLE BELGE

74.

"Keep all Canadians busy.
Buy 1918 Victory Bonds."

Canadian poster.

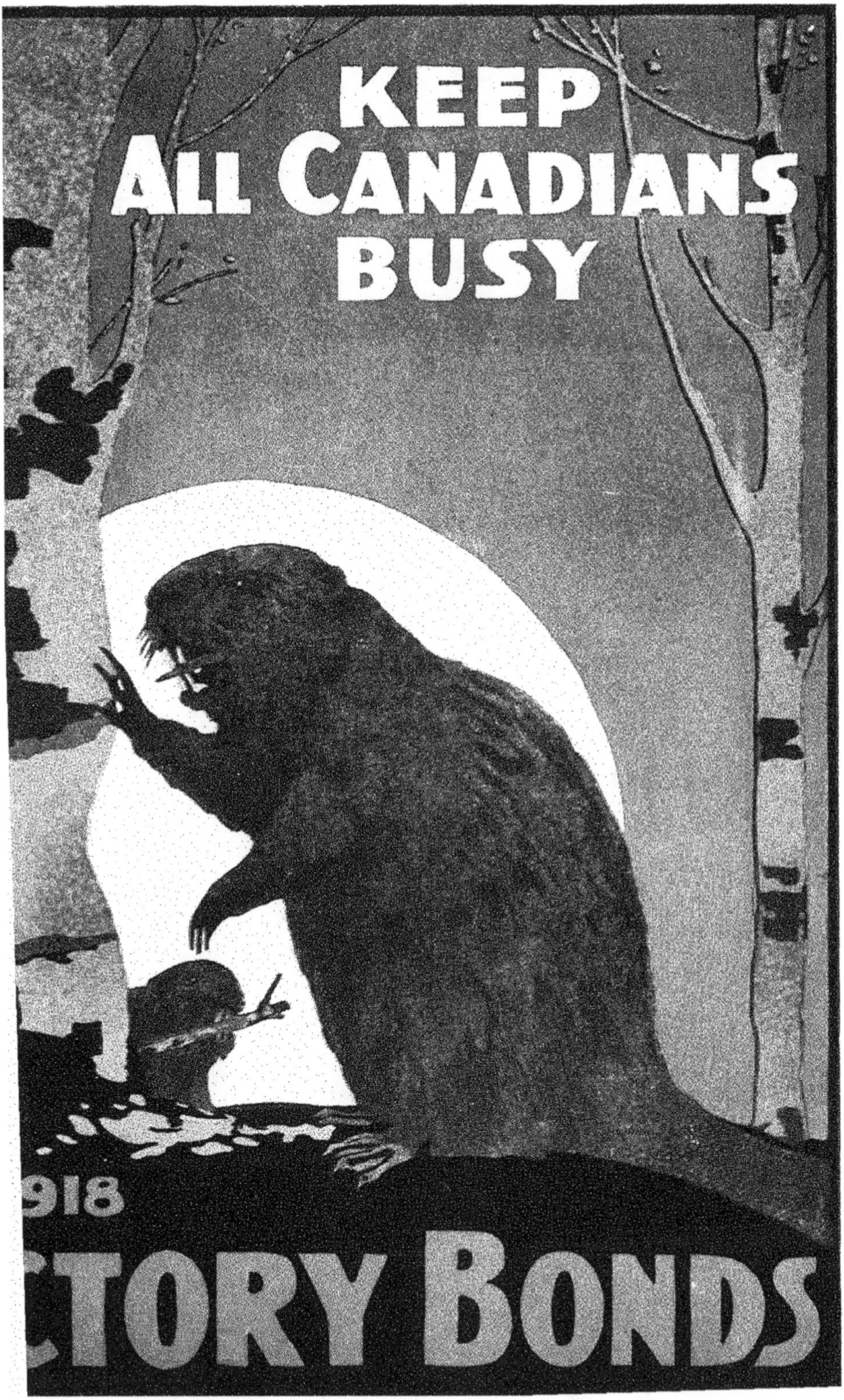
KEEP
ALL CANADIANS
BUSY
918
CTORY BONDS

75.

LOUIS RAEMAEKERS.

"Neutral America and the Hun."

Poster of an Exhibition of Raemaekers cartoons in Milan.

OSIZIONE RAEMAEKERS

ESENTE DA BOLLO

76.

V. PREISSIG.

"CZECHOSLOVAKS! JOIN OUR FREE COLOURS"

One of six recruiting posters issued by the Czechoslovak
Recruiting Office, New York, U.S.A., 1918.

Printed at the Wentworth Institute, Boston, U S A.

CPSIA information can be obtained
at www.ICGtesting.com
Printed in the USA
BVHW040916050219
539516BV00009B/356/P